The Quotable Investor

The Quotable
Investor

EDITED BY
SANFORD JACOBS

FOREWORD BY
PAUL VOLCKER

The Lyons Press
Guilford, CT
An Imprint of Globe Pequot Press

FIRST EDITION

Printed in United States of America

10 9 8 7 6 5 4 3 2 1

Library of Congress Cataloging-in-Publication Data is available on file.

Contents

Foreword

I have a confession to make. I'm a cautious man, always braced for the worst, seeing a dark cloud behind every silver lining. Those traits haven't served me well in the last decade. It's not that I've lost money investing, at least not on balance. But I couldn't share the unbridled ebullience (or the financial returns) of men and women less than half my age, with half a dozen years at best on Wall Street.

That's not been good for my ego. But I've been immensely cheered night after night by thumbing through THE QUOTABLE INVESTOR before passing into blissful sleep. Right there, in black and white, is the distilled wisdom of the ages about the twists and turns of investment fate. From Greek philosophers right up through Peter Lynch and Warren Buffett, it's all laid out, concisely, eloquently, even sometimes poetically: the need to maintain caution, to keep a skeptical eye, to resist mass folly for long-term investment success.

Markets fluctuate, just as J. P. Morgan famously replied at the beginning of the twentieth century when asked for his own forecast of stock prices.

> *"Time and again emotion moves markets more than rational analysis. Common sense and due care make for better investment decisions than following fads or sticking a pin in the stock tables."*

> *"There are booms, there are busts. And the excesses in either direction are never all that apparent until too late."*

> *"Money is nice to have, but it's not a guarantee of happiness."*

I think I knew all that already. As the saying goes, a pessimist is an optimist with experience, and I have by now had quite a bit of that. But I wonder about all those who have been riding the bull market, with so much success and élan, all their young adult lives.

I don't want to disturb their success and their pleasure. They will find there is more than enough wit in this little book to entertain even if they think the lessons aren't really relevant in the Internet age. As for me, I like both the wit and the wisdom.

—Paul Volcker

Introduction

Happily, in doing this book I could select from a rich lode of quotations, from sources ancient and new. After all, investing and all that attaches to it—risk, profit, loss, wealth, greed, money—have excited people for millennia. More than 400 years before Christ, Sophocles railed, "Of evils current upon earth, the worst is money"; and Aristophanes wryly observed, "I am amazed that anyone who has made a fortune should send for his friends." Nowadays, the fortune maker brags to a chat room or bulletin board on an Internet investor site.

Thanks in large measure to the spread of 401(k) retirement plans, discount brokerage houses, the computer and the Internet, investing has become a national pastime. Nearly half of the 100 million households in the United States own stocks. Youngsters learn stock-simulation games in high school, but not Shakespeare. (They know the Motley Fool as an investor Website.) The market chatter of CNBC and CNNfn plays across television sets in homes, restaurants, bars, and health clubs across the country.

The cliché that Wall Street has come to Main Street is finally true. Except, few people live near a road called Main Street and our fathers' Wall Street, of full-service brokers and fixed-by-fiat charges for buying and selling shares has been transformed. Now, we pay a relative pittance to buy and sell shares. We can track our portfolios effortlessly and easily troll for stocks, using sophisticated computer programs, which in the past were available only to the pros.

While most of us are content to let mutual funds invest for us, millions are doing it themselves at online trading firms. Like slot machines, online trading has become an obsession for thousands of people. They spend hours on the Web, screening stocks and scouring chat rooms for the next Big One. Often they risk too much, borrowing through margin accounts to inflate their purchasing power. "Trading is addictive," 36-year-old, stay-at-home mom Paula Stringham told the *Wall Street Journal* in 2000, when her husband covered a $2,900 margin call for her, on a promise she would curtail her trading. "I wish I could go back to 1999 . . . and never day-trade and never get myself into this mess."

In collecting these quotations, I had great pleasure from reading through a lot of amusing, interesting, and sometimes instructive material. In the midst of my efforts, the stock market went through some stomach-churning gyrations, showing us once again that what goes up still can and will come down. I wasn't immune from having my modest stock holdings punished by the collapse, but I was rewarded with some pungent expressions from the news coverage.

For the sake of full disclosure: I had a rewarding and happy 25-year career at Dow Jones, but I have not consciously favored the *Wall Street Journal*, where I was a writer for nearly 20 years, or other Dow Jones publications, such as *Barron's*, *SmartMoney*, or its Websites. But they, and the *New York Times*, probably have more credits than any other sources.

The Quotable Investor

1

The Many Ways
We Play the Market

The bullish investor, fascinated by his or her individual success, may have great difficulty in valuing anything other than growth.

TAD CRAWFORD
FOREWORD TO *ONCE IN GOLCONDA*, BY JOHN BROOKS

Eighty percent of success is showing up.

WOODY ALLEN

Some people have built-in filters that screen out the boos and amplify the hurrahs. Those are the people who never know when they're in trouble.

TOMMY DAVIS, VENTURE CAPITALIST
FROM ROGER VON OECH'S *THE JUDGE*

It's not the bulls and bears you need to avoid—it's the bum steers.

CHUCK HILLIS

The optimist proclaims that we live in the best of all possible worlds; and the pessimist fears this is true.

JAMES BRANCH CABELL (1879–1958)
THE SILVER STALLION (1926)

———•◦•———

The place where optimism most flourishes is the lunatic asylum.

HAVELOCK ELLIS
THE DANCE OF LIFE (1923)

I told them this is not the end of the bull market.

JEFFREY M. APPLEGATE, CHIEF U.S. STRATEGIST,
LEHMAN BROTHERS, AFTER NASDAQ FELL 25.3 PERCENT
THE WEEK OF APRIL 10, 2000

———◆••◆———

In any bear market, you have pockets that go against the market. I've made quite a bit of money in bear markets, in special areas.

GEORGE SOROS, LEGENDARY HEDGE FUND OPERATOR

To worship the bull is to worship the abundance and fertility of the divine.

TAD CRAWFORD
FOREWORD TO ONCE IN GOLCONDA BY JOHN BROOKS

———•·•·•———

Bears don't live on Park Avenue.

BERNARD BARUCH (1870–1965)

Bulls make money. Bears make money. Pigs get slaughtered.

WALL STREET ADAGE

——•◦•◦•——

Wall Street has a uniquely hysterical way of thinking the world will end tomorrow but be fully recovered in the long run, then a few years later believing the immediate future is rosy, but the long term stinks.

KENNETH L. FISHER
WALL STREET WALTZ

Bull markets have no resistance—bear markets have no support.

ANONYMOUS

When lambs turn into bulls, owls suffer.

STEVE LEUTHOLD, CHAIRMAN OF THE LEUTHOLD GROUP,
AN INVESTMENT ADVISORY FIRM, AND AUTHOR OF
THE MYTHS OF INFLATION AND INVESTING

Happy is the man who learns from the misfortunes of others.

AESOP'S FABLES
THE LION, THE FOX AND THE ASS

Like an oversexed guy in a whorehouse. This is the time to start investing.

WARREN BUFFETT TO *FORBES* MAGAZINE, OCTOBER 1974,
DURING PROLONGED BEAR MARKET
FROM RALPH WANGER'S *A ZEBRA IN LION COUNTRY*

Warren Buffet, the greatest investor of them all, looks for the same sorts of opportunities I do, except that when he finds them, he buys the whole company.

PETER LYNCH
ONE UP ON WALL STREET

Our policy is to concentrate holdings. We try to avoid buying a little of this or that when we are only luke-warm about the business or its price. When we are convinced as to attractiveness, we believe in buying worthwhile amounts.

WARREN BUFFETT
LETTER TO BERKSHIRE HATHAWAY SHAREHOLDERS (1978)

Who against hope believed in hope.

ROMANS 4:18

As a very successful investor once said: "The bearish argument always sounds more intelligent."

PETER LYNCH
ONE UP ON WALL STREET

———◆••◆———

Hope says to us constantly, "Go on, go on."

MADAME DE MAINTENON (1635–1719),
SECOND WIFE OF LOUIS XIV

More are taken in by hope than by cunning.

LUC DE CLAPIERS VAUVENARGUES
REFLECTIONS AND MAXIMS (CA. 1747)

In matters financial, M. Grandet . . . [combined] the characteristics of the Bengal tiger and the boa constrictor. . . . No man could see the man pass without feeling a certain kind of admiration, which was half dread, half respect.

HONORÉ DE BALZAC (1799–1850)
EUGÉNIE GRANDET (1833)

The problem with the person who thinks he's a long-term investor and impervious to short-term gyrations is that the emotion of fear and pain will eventually make him sell badly.

ROBERT WIBBELSMAN, PORTFOLIO MANAGER
AT STROME SUSSKIND

———•◦•◦•———

We select our marketable equity securities in much the same way we would evaluate a business for acquisition in its entirety. We want the business to be (1) one that we can understand, (2) with favorable long-term prospects, (3) operated by honest and competent people, and (4) available at a very attractive price.

WARREN BUFFETT
LETTER TO BERKSHIRE HATHAWAY INC. SHAREHOLDERS (1977)

It will fluctuate.

> J. P. MORGAN'S ANSWER TO A REPORTER
> WHEN ASKED WHAT THE MARKET WILL DO.
> FROM JOHN BROOKS'S *ONCE IN GOLCONDA* (1969)

I seen my opportunities and I took 'em.

> GEORGE WASHINGTON PLUNKITT (1842–1924)
> QUOTED IN WILLIAM L. RIORDON'S *PLUNKITT*
> *OF TAMMANY HALL* (1905)

Investing calls for much the same qualities as those required to become a first-class ballet dancer or concert pianist.

JOHN TRAIN
THE MIDAS TOUCH

———•◦•◦•———

We will never buy anything we don't understand.

WARREN BUFFETT, FROM HIS OFT-REPEATED RESPONSE
WHEN ASKED WHY HE DOESN'T BUY HIGH-TECH STOCKS

———•◦•◦•———

What better way to prove that you understand a subject than to make money out of it?

HAROLD ROSENBERG (1906–1978)

It is strange the way the ignorant and inexperienced so often and so undeservedly succeed when the informed and the experienced fail.

MARK TWAIN
AUTOBIOGRAPHY OF MARK TWAIN;
MARK TWAIN IN ERUPTION

Seize the day, put no trust in the morrow.

HORACE (65–8 B.C.)
ODES BOOK XI, LAST LINE

Never let yesterday use up too much of today.

WILL ROGERS

You should assume everything you read online is false until you can confirm it somewhere else.

JOHN STARK, CHIEF OF THE SEC'S
OFFICE OF INTERNET ENFORCEMENT
FROM *THE WALL STREET JOURNAL
INTERACTIVE EDITION'S COMPLETE GUIDE
TO BECOMING A SUCCESSFUL INTERNET INVESTOR* (2000)

To the rash and impetuous stock player, my advice is: Forget Wall Street and take your mad money to Hialeah, Monte Carlo, Saratoga, Nassau, Santa Anita, or Baden-Baden. At least in those . . . surroundings when you lose, you'll be able to say you had a great time doing it.

PETER LYNCH
ONE UP ON WALL STREET

Men, it has been well said, think in herds; it will be seen that they go mad in herds, while they only recover their senses slowly, and one by one.

CHARLES MACKAY
*EXTRAORDINARY POPULAR DELUSIONS
AND THE MADNESS OF CROWDS* (1852)

The general public has not by and large taken Economics 101, and those who did sit through it have probably forgotten much of what they learned.

ROBERT J. SHILLER
IRRATIONAL EXUBERANCE

"100,000 lemmings can't be wrong."

GRAFFITO QUOTED IN JONATHAN CLEMENTS'S
"GETTING GOING" COLUMN
THE WALL STREET JOURNAL (JULY 18, 2000)

Buffett, like most successful investors, particularly of the "value" school, begins by purging himself of emotion and substituting intellect.

JOHN TRAIN
THE MIDAS TOUCH (1988)

2

The Market, Wall Street, and Appurtenances

Finance is the art of passing currency from hand to hand until it finally disappears.

ROBERT W. SARNOFF (1918–1997)
CHAIRMAN OF RCA CORP.

———•••———

One of the troubles with Wall Street is that people either feel it's "impossible" or they figure it's "easy."

JOHN MAGEE
WALL STREET—MAIN STREET—AND YOU (1972)

One must remember that the stock market is as unsentimental as the weather report.

B. MARCHAND SAGE
STREET FIGHTING AT WALL AND BROAD:
AN INSIDER'S TALE OF MANIPULATION (1980)

———◆•◆•◆———

Profit has always been a primary concern of Wall Street. For some, profit is an evil word, but for most of Wall Street, profits are why they are here.

GERALD APPEL, PRESIDENT OF SIGNALERT,
AN INVESTMENT MANAGEMENT FIRM

Wall Street is motivated primarily by emotions—fear and greed.

WALL STREET ADAGE

The stock market—the daytime adventure serial of the well-to-do—would not be the stock market if it did not have its ups and downs.

JOHN BROOKS
BUSINESS ADVENTURES (1969)

"Wall Street," reads the sinister old gag, "is a street with a river at one end and a graveyard at the other."

This is striking, but incomplete. It omits the kindergarten in the middle.

FREDRICK SCHWED JR.
WHERE ARE THE CUSTOMERS' YACHTS?
FROM MICHAEL LEWIS'S *LIAR'S POKER* (1990)

Consider the myth that brokerage firms come in categories that define the services they offer—like "discount," "full commission" and "on-line." If you look closely, you'll see that these categories don't exist anymore. Competition has wiped them out.

DAVE POTTRUCK, CO-CEO OF CHARLES SCHWAB CORP.
AND AUTHOR OF *WALL STREET'S WAKE-UP CALL:*
SERVING EMPOWERED INVESTORS
SPEECH AT SECURITIES INDUSTRY ASSOCIATION
ANNUAL MEETING, NOVEMBER 5, 1999

A market is a combined behavior of thousands of people responding to information, misinformation, and whim.

KENNETH CHANG

The market is not an invention of capitalism. It has existed for centuries. It is an invention of civilization.

MIKHAIL GORBACHEV

Capitalism without bankruptcy is like Christianity without hell.

FRANK BORMAN, CHIEF EXECUTIVE OFFICER
FOR THE NOW BANKRUPT EASTERN AIRLINES

The difference between playing the stock market and the horses is that one of the horses must win.

JOEY ADAMS

———•••••———

I do not regard a broker as a member of the human race.

HONORÉ DE BALZAC (1799–1850)

Show people tend to treat their finances like their dentistry. They assume the man handling it knows what he's doing.

DICK CAVETT, ON THE INVESTIGATION
OF HIS INVESTMENT BROKER

I don't know how much money I've got. . . . I did ask the accountant how much it came to. I wrote it down on a bit of paper. But I've lost the paper.

JOHN LENNON (1940–1980)

Is it not odd that the only generous person I ever knew, who had money to be generous with, should be a stock-broker?

PERCY BYSSHE SHELLEY

———•·•·•———

It's my bet that the recommending brokers were playing the "bigger fool" theory. It holds that you might be a fool to pay more for a company than it seems worth, but you don't need to worry because there will always be a bigger fool willing to pay more.

ALAN LECHNER, FORMER RESEARCH DIRECTOR
AT BROKERAGE FIRM STIFEL NICOLAUS & CO.

"Broker": the end-result of turning a large fortune into a small one.

KURT BROUWER
UNUSUAL INVESTMENT DEFINITIONS (1987)

A financier is a pawnbroker with imagination.

SIR ARTHUR WING PINERO (1855–1934)

I have never been satisfied that markets are rational. It is not my experience.

ROBERT SHILLER
NEW YORK TIMES, APRIL 30, 2000

Everyone has the brainpower to follow the stock market. If you made it through fifth-grade math, you can do it.

PETER LYNCH
MODERN MATURITY MAGAZINE (JANUARY/FEBRUARY 1995)

———•◦•◦•———

Eventually, every stock can only be worth the value of the cash flow it is able to earn for the benefit of investors. In the final analysis true value will win out.

BURTON G. MALKIEL
WALL STREET JOURNAL EDITORIAL PAGE, APRIL 14, 2000.

I have probably purchased fifty "hot tips" in my career, maybe even more. When I put them all together, I know I am a net loser.

CHARLES SCHWAB

———•·••·•———

Twenty-four years ago, when I ran for Congress, for good or ill, I made the decision that in order to avoid even the appearance of any conflict of interest, on the many subjects that would come up for voters, I decided as a matter of personal policy I would not invest in stocks. Now, missing the bull market is not the greatest thing in the world, financially. But for me, it was the right decision.

AL GORE, STATEMENT TO REPORTERS
DURING HIS UNSUCCESSFUL PRESIDENTIAL CAMPAIGN, MAY 17, 2000

Ninety percent of the people in the stock market, professionals and amateurs alike, simply haven't done enough homework.

WILLIAM J. O'NEIL, FOUNDER
OF *INVESTOR'S BUSINESS DAILY*

———•••———

Over the last 100 years, aggregate stock prices have either gone up too much or down too much.

ROBERT SHILLER
NEW YORK TIMES, APRIL 30, 2000

I've always thought that there was very little wit wanted to make a fortune in the City [London's financial district].

ANTHONY TROLLOPE (1815–1852)

———•◦•◦•———

Never before have so many unskilled twenty-four-year-olds made so much money in so little time as we did this decade [the 1980s] in New York and London.

MICHAEL LEWIS
LIAR'S POKER (1990)

WALL STREET, n. A symbol for sin for every devil to re-buke. That Wall Street is a den of thieves is a belief that serves every unsuccessful thief in place of a hope in Heaven.

> AMBROSE BIERCE (1842–1914)
> *THE DEVIL'S DICTIONARY* (1911)

———

Yet one fine day . . . *just like that,* this very phrase had bubbled up into his brain. On Wall Street he and a few others—how many?—three hundred, four hundred, five hundred?—had become precisely that . . . Masters of the Universe.

> TOM WOLFE
> *THE BONFIRE OF THE VANITIES* (1987)

The men on the trading floor may not have been to school, but they have Ph.D.s in man's ignorance. In any market, as in any poker game, there is a fool.

MICHAEL LEWIS
LIAR'S POKER (1990)

Never look to a bond trader for economic advice.

REAGAN ADMINISTRATION TREASURY SECRETARY DONALD REGAN,
WALL STREET JOURNAL, JUNE 1, 1981

They aim more at increasing their profits than at lessening radical swings in stock prices.

FINDINGS OF A 1963 SEC STUDY
OF NEW YORK STOCK EXCHANGE SPECIALISTS

Front running in its broadest sense is nothing more than trading on the basis of information about impending market transactions that the public doesn't know about. It's all a big no-no and against the rules. It's also widely practiced.

PAUL GIBSON
BEAR TRAP

If investments are keeping you awake at night—sell down to the sleeping point.

ANONYMOUS WALL STREET SAYING

Money often costs too much.

RALPH WALDO EMERSON

Things are almost never clear on Wall Street, or when they are, then it's too late to profit from them.

PETER LYNCH
ONE UP ON WALL STREET

In the book of things people more often do wrong than right, investing must certainly top the list, followed closely by wallpapering and eating artichokes.

ROBERT KLEIN, COMEDIAN

Avoid the roller coaster of worry by *not* checking your stock prices in the paper every day. How often do you check on the value of your home?

ANONYMOUS WALL STREET ADAGE

Never check stock prices on Friday—it could spoil your weekend.

ANONYMOUS WALL STREET ADVICE

Portfolio diversification makes up for investor ignorance.

WALL STREET ADAGE

Every investor should be prepared financially and psychologically for the possibility of poor short-term results.

BENJAMIN GRAHAM (1896–1976)

———•••———

Timidity prompted by past failures causes investors to miss the most important bull markets.

WALTER SCHLOSS, VALUE INVESTOR WHO LEARNED FROM BENJAMIN GRAHAM

———•••———

No tree grows to the sky.

ANONYMOUS WALL STREET ADAGE

Never hold on to a loser just to collect the dividends.

ANONYMOUS WALL STREET ADAGE

Unless you can watch your stock holdings decline by 50 percent without becoming panic-stricken, you should not be in the stock market.

WARREN BUFFETT

Don't wait until the time or the market is just right to start investing—start now. The best time to plant an oak tree was 20 years ago—the second best time is now.

JAMES STOWERS JR., BILLIONAIRE FOUNDER OF AMERICAN CENTURY MUTUAL FUNDS

An investment strategy is not worth much if you constantly change due to a lack of underlying confidence or comfort. This is the difference between investing and playing the market.

PETER SKIRKANICH, PORTFOLIO MANAGER OF
$1.8 BILLION-ASSET FOX INVESTMENTS

A stock does not know that you own it.

PETER LYNCH
ONE UP ON WALL STREET

There will always be bull markets followed by bear markets followed by bull markets.

JOHN TEMPLETON

———•◦•◦•———

I'm glad it wasn't two pennies. We'd be underground.

JIM SINEGAL, COSTCO'S CHIEF EXECUTIVE,
AFTER THE FIRM REPORTED QUARTER PROFIT
ONE CENT BELOW WALL STREET ESTIMATES AND
ITS STOCK FELL 22 PERCENT.
WALL STREET JOURNAL, MAY 25, 2000

———•◦•◦•———

I realized every television [at New York's JFK International Airport immigration line] was showing CNBC. Imagine, that's about the very first thing every tourist sees when he comes into this country.

EDWARD YARDENI, CHIEF ECONOMIST,
DEUTSCHE BANK SECURITIES
FROM JAMES M. PETHOKOUKIS'S "MARKET MANIA"
U.S. NEWS & WORLD REPORT, APRIL 3, 2000

Honesty will never be a profit center on Wall Street, but the brokers used to keep up appearances. Now they have stopped pretending.

JAMES GRANT
FINANCIAL TIMES, JULY 19, 1999

———•••••———

The study of market behavior belongs to anthropology as much as it does to economics.

JOHN TRAIN
THE MIDAS TOUCH (1988)

3

The Economy Stirs It All

Capitalism is the astounding belief that the most wicked of men will do the most wicked of things for the greatest good of everyone.

JOHN MAYNARD KEYNES (1883–1946)

In every well-governed state wealth is a sacred thing; in democracies it is the *only* sacred thing.

ANATOLE FRANCE (1844–1924)

Innovation is the specific instrument of entrepreneurship . . . the act that endows resources with a new capacity to create wealth.

PETER DRUCKER, AUTHOR AND CONSULTANT

We have always known that heedless self-interest was bad morals; we know now that it is bad economics.

FRANKLIN DELANO ROOSEVELT
SECOND INAUGURAL ADDRESS, JANUARY 20, 1937

We should always remind ourselves that capitalism, now politely called the market system, has always, basically, been unstable.

JOHN KENNETH GALBRAITH
LOS ANGELES TIMES, DECEMBER 12, 1999

Economics is the study of how men and society *choose*, with or without the use of money, to employ *scarce* productive resources to produce various commodities over time and distribute them for consumption, now and in the future, among various people and groups of society.

PAUL A. SAMUELSON, PROFESSOR OF ECONOMICS
AT MIT, WINNER OF 1970 NOBEL PRIZE IN
ECONOMICS (1961)

Most of the economics as taught is a form of brain damage.

ERNST F. SCHUMACHER
THE READER, MARCH 25, 1977

[E]conomics is helplessly behind the times, and unable to handle its subject matter in a way to entitle it to standing as a modern science.

THORSTEIN VEBLEN (1857–1929)
THE PLACE OF SCIENCE IN MODERN CIVILISATION,
AND OTHER ESSAYS (1919)

None of us really understands what's going on with all these numbers.

DAVID STOCKMAN, U.S. BUDGET DIRECTOR, 1981

If one could divine the nature of the economic forces in the world, one could foretell the future.

ROBERT L. HEILBRONER

Economic growth is not only unnecessary, but ruinous.

ALEXANDER SOLZHENITSYN

As the economy gets better, everything else gets worse.

ART BUCHWALD

The American experience indicates that the major business cycle has had an average duration of a little over eight years.

ALVIN H. HANSEN
FISCAL POLICY AND BUSINESS CYCLES (1941)

The instability of the economy is equaled only by the instability of economists.

JOHN HENRY WILLIAMS
NEW YORK TIMES, JUNE 2, 1956

Inflation is repudiation.

CALVIN COOLIDGE (1872–1933)

Nothing good can be said for a rapid rise in prices.

PAUL A. SAMUELSON
ECONOMICS (1961)

The engine which drives Enterprise is not Thrift, but Profit.

JOHN MAYNARD KEYNES (1883–1946)
A TREATISE ON MONEY (1930)

Capitalism, it is said, is a system wherein man exploits man. And communism—is vice versa.

DANIEL BELL (1919–   )
THE END OF IDEOLOGY (1960)

If you can count your money, you don't have a billion dollars.

J. PAUL GETTY

Dollars have never been known to produce character, and character will never be produced by money.

W. K. KELLOGG (1860–1951)

The individual serves the industrial system not by supplying it with savings and the resulting capital; he serves it by consuming its products.

JOHN KENNETH GALBRAITH
THE NEW INDUSTRIAL STATE (1967)

Americans want action for their money. They are fascinated by its self-reproducing qualities if it's put to work. . . .

PAULA NELSON

———•••••———

[T]here are some extremely useful things to be learned in Economics 101. The most useful is probably the concept that true wealth accrues to price fixing beyond any other business practice.

BENJAMIN J. STEIN
A LICENSE TO STEAL (1992)

4

Dot-com Mania
and Other Popular Delusions

Anyone can get rich these days by starting a business and selling equity, so long as the firm's name has a dot-com in it.

DAVID LEVY, ECONOMIST, JEROME LEVY INSTITUTE
QUOTED IN *BARRON'S*, November 30, 1998

———•••••———

Young men have a passion for regarding their elders as senile.

HENRY BROOKS ADAMS (1838–1918)
THE EDUCATION OF HENRY ADAMS (1907)

We have actually seen a few failures. Believe me, we will see more than half the dot-coms fail. But that doesn't mean the Internet is not a tremendous opportunity.

MARY MODAHL, VICE PRESIDENT OF RESEARCH,
FORRESTER RESEARCH
WALL STREET JOURNAL, JULY 17, 2000

The effect of these technologies could rival and arguably even surpass the impact the telegraph had prior to, and just after, the Civil War.

ALAN GREENSPAN, FEDERAL RESERVE CHAIRMAN
U.S. NEWS & WORLD REPORT, JUNE 19, 2000

The Nasdaq mania has shattered the hierarchy of Wall Street, with the professionals forced to abdicate authority to amateurs.

RON CHERNOW
NEW YORK TIMES, APRIL 16, 2000

In this new world, companies like Apple Computer could go from the garage to a billion dollars of sales in the matter of a couple of years.

RICHARD DRIEHAUS, OF THE MONEY MANAGEMENT FIRM
DRIEHAUS CAPITAL MANAGEMENT
BARRON'S, FEBRUARY 21, 2000

At least temporarily, the ghost of Isaac Newton has revisited the Nasdaq Stock Market.

> BURTON G. MALKIEL ON THE NASDAQ INDEX'S
> MORE THAN 22 PERCENT PLUNGE FROM ITS MARCH 10 PEAK
> *WALL STREET JOURNAL*, APRIL 14, 2000

The numbers clearly show the Darwinian process at work in the Internet. The weak falter, while the strong surge ahead.

> GREG KYLE, PRESIDENT, PEGASUS RESEARCH INTERNATIONAL
> *BARRON'S*, JUNE 19, 2000

Last year the market was so euphoric and exuberant that it was looking for any excuse to buy, and a press release was a good one. Now the market is looking for any excuse to sell.

HENRY BLODGET, MERRILL LYNCH ANALYST
WALL STREET JOURNAL, MAY 24, 2000

It is the business of the future to be dangerous; and it is among the merits of science that it equips the future for its duties.

ALFRED NORTH WHITEHEAD (1861–1947)

I never thought the Nasdaq would drop 35 percent in 15 days.

> STANLEY DRUCKENMILLER, TOP MANAGER
> OF GEORGE SOROS'S HEDGE FUNDS
> REUTERS NEWS SERVICE, APRIL 28, 2000

Many [Internet] companies were just figments of Wall Street's overly vivid imagination.

> CHARLES SCAVONE, MANAGER, THE $894 MILLION AIM
> SMALL CAP OPPORTUNITIES FUND
> WALL STREET JOURNAL, JULY 10, 2000

Of course I feel sorry for the investors. But at the same time, they're all qualified professionals and in a position to understand the risks in a deal.

PATRICK HEDELIN, CHIEF FINANCIAL OFFICER OF BOO.COM,
AN INTERNET FASHION RETAILER THAT WENT BROKE
AFTER BURNING UP $135 MILLION OF START-UP FUNDING
WALL STREET JOURNAL, JUNE 27, 2000

The only way to make money buying overpriced stocks is if they become more overpriced.

MICHAEL METZ, CHIEF EQUITY STRATEGIST, CIBC OPPENHEIMER

Internet pure play companies, including Amazon.com, are extremely volatile. I think that is highly unlikely to change any time in the near future.

AMAZON.COM FOUNDER AND CHIEF EXECUTIVE JEFF BEZOS
AT COMPANY'S MAY 18, 1999, ANNUAL MEETING

———•••••———

As the [tulip] mania increased, prices augmented, until, in the year 1635, many persons were known to invest a fortune of 100,000 florins in the purchase of 40 roots.

CHARLES MACKAY
EXTRAORDINARY POPULAR DELUSIONS
& THE MADNESS OF CROWDS (1852)

What matters for a stock market boom is not, however, the reality of the Internet revolution, which is hard to discern, but rather the *public impressions* that the revolution creates.

> ROBERT J. SHILLER
> *IRRATIONAL EXUBERANCE* (2000)

The ensuing migration . . . into the financial district resembles the famous gold rush to the Klondike, with the not unimportant difference that there really was gold in the Klondike.

> BENJAMIN GRAHAM AND DAVID DODD
> *SECURITY ANALYSIS* (1934)

The rage for possessing them [tulips] soon caught the middle classes of society, and merchants and shopkeepers, even of moderate means, began to vie with each other in the rarity of these flowers and the preposterous prices paid for them. A trader at Harlem was known to pay one-half of his fortune for a single root. . . .

CHARLES MACKAY
EXTRAORDINARY POPULAR DELUSIONS
& THE MADNESS OF CROWDS (1852)

Any person given to excessive optimism should step back to 1637, the wonderful year when all the sober and somber people of Holland believed you could get rich on tulip bulbs. Call it tulipmania. In Holland its seventeenth century residents did not get rich on tulips or anything else.

JOHN KENNETH GALBRAITH
LOS ANGELES TIMES, DECEMBER 12, 1999

That's good for our system, and that in fact, with all of its hype and craziness, is something that, at the end of the day, probably is more plus than minus.

ALAN GREENSPAN, FEDERAL RESERVE CHAIRMAN
TELLING THE SENATE BUDGET COMMITTEE THE BENEFIT
OF INVESTORS' WILLINGNESS TO BUY INTERNET STOCKS
WASHINGTON POST, JANUARY 29, 1999

Right now we are in the most dangerous time in financial history . . . the greatest financial bubble of all times.

SIR JOHN TEMPLETON, FOUNDER OF THE TEMPLETON GROWTH FUND
BUSINESS WEEK, JULY 3, 2000

One has the feeling this will end badly. It may be the greatest slaughter of naifs since the Children's Crusade.

RALPH WANGER, ACORN FUND PORTFOLIO MANAGER,
COMMENTING ON MINDLESS SPECULATION
IN PROFITLESS INTERNET COMPANIES
U.S. NEWS & WORLD REPORT, APRIL 3, 2000

Teenage chat and drivel purchased the most powerful media company on the face of the earth.

JOHN SVIOKLA, CONSULTANT AT DIAMOND TECHNOLOGY PARTNERS,
COMMENTING ON AMERICA ONLINE'S PURCHASE OF TIME WARNER
WALL STREET JOURNAL, JULY 10, 2000

I can't believe I'm buying investment advice from the ice-machine repair guy.

CHRIS ANDERSON, UPON LEARNING THAT WEB SITE ANALYST
WHOSE ADVICE HE FOLLOWS, "DR. WALL STREET," IS A STUDENT
WITH A SUMMER JOB MAINTAINING ICE MACHINES
WALL STREET JOURNAL, JULY 10, 2000

———————

If the automobile had followed the same development as the computer, a Rolls Royce would today cost one hundred dollars, get a million miles per gallon, and explode once a year, killing everyone inside.

ROBERT CRINGELY
INFO WORLD

5

Money, Money, Money

Everything is worth what its purchaser will pay for it.

PUBLILIUS SYRUS (FIRST CENTURY B.C.)
MAXIM 847

Money does not motivate but only for a short time and only as long as it serves as a measure of worth or of power or of victory.

JAMES HAYES

No one can doubt that the American people remain susceptible to the speculative mood—to the conviction that enterprise can be attended by unlimited rewards in which they, individually, were meant to share. A rising market can still bring the reality of riches, this, in turn, can draw more and more people to participate.

JOHN KENNETH GALBRAITH
THE GREAT CRASH OF 1929 (1954 EDITION)

———

Money is a handmaiden if thou knowest how to use it; a mistress if thou knowest not.

HORACE (65–68 B.C.)

Liking money like I like it, is nothing less than mysticism. Money is a glory.

SALVADOR DALI, PAINTER

Money, it turned out, was exactly like sex; you thought of nothing else if you didn't have it and thought of other things if you did.

JAMES BALDWIN (1924–1987)
NOBODY KNOWS MY NAME (1961)

Marry for money, my little sonny,
a rich man's joke is always funny.

HEBREW PROVERB

The three most serious losses which a man can suffer are those affecting money, health and reputation. Loss of money is far the worst.

SAMUEL BUTLER (1835–1902)
THE WAY OF ALL FLESH (1903)

Marriage, like money, is still with us; and, like money, progressively devalued.

ROBERT GRAVES

Invest at least as much time and effort in choosing a new stock as you would in choosing a new refrigerator.

PETER LYNCH
ONE UP ON WALL STREET

It is an almost unbelievable fact that Wall Street never asks, "How much is this business selling for?"

BENJAMIN GRAHAM AND DAVID L. DODD
SECURITY ANALYSIS (1934)

———●·●·●———

The truth is, growth stocks don't always grow.

MONEY MAGAZINE, JUNE 2000

———●·●·●———

The Golden Rule of Investing: Know Your Source.

ADVERTISEMENT FOR MORGAN STANLEY DEAN WITTER/ONLINE

Speculation on a large scale requires a pervasive sense of confidence and optimism and conviction that ordinary people were meant to be rich.

JOHN KENNETH GALBRAITH
THE GREAT CRASH OF 1929 (1954 EDITION)

———•••———

If Karl, instead of writing a lot about capital had made a lot of it . . . it would have been much better.

KARL MARX'S MOTHER

Of evils current upon earth, the worst is money. Money 'tis that sacks cities, and drives men forth from hearth and home; warps and seduces native innocence, and breeds a habit of dishonesty.

SOPHOCLES (C. 496–406 B.C.)
ANTIGONE

To be clever enough to get a great deal of money, one must be stupid enough to want it.

G. K. CHESTERTON (1874–1936)

We are told that the love of money is the root of all evil; but money itself is one of the most useful contrivances ever invented: it is not its fault that some people are foolish . . . or miserly enough to be fonder of it than of their own souls.

GEORGE BERNARD SHAW (1856–1950)
THE INTELLIGENT WOMAN'S GUIDE TO SOCIALISM, CAPITALISM, SOVIETISM AND FASCISM

———————

Money is the root of all evil, and yet it is such a useful root that we cannot get on without it any more than we can without potatoes.

LOUISA MAY ALCOTT

Money can't buy friends, but you can get a better class of enemy.

SPIKE MULLIGAN

Money is like manure. You have to spread it around or it smells.

J. PAUL GETTY (1892–1976)

The rich man glories in his riches, because he feels that they naturally draw upon him the attention of the world. . . . At the thought of this, his heart seems to swell and dilate itself within him, and he is fonder of his wealth, upon this account, than for all the other advantages it procures him.

ADAM SMITH (1723–1790)
THEORY OF MORAL SENTIMENTS

Everything in the world may be endured except continued prosperity.

JOHANN WOLFGANG VON GOETHE (1749–1832)

After a certain point, money is meaningless. It ceases to be the goal. The game is what counts.

ARISTOTLE ONASSIS (1906–1975)

Money was never a big motivation for me, except as a way to keep score. The real excitement is playing the game.

DONALD TRUMP

If you want to know what God thinks of money, just look at some of the people He gave it to.

DOROTHY PARKER (1893–1967)

Money . . . is the string with which a sardonic destiny directs the motions of its puppets.

SOMERSET MAUGHAM

Almost any man knows how to earn money, but not one in a million knows how to spend it.

HENRY DAVID THOREAU

When it is a question of money, everybody is of the same religion.

VOLTAIRE (1694–1778)

———•·•·•———

Nobody knew better how to dictate liberality to others; but her love of money was equal to her love of directing, and she knew quite as well how to save her own as to spend that of her friends.

JANE AUSTEN (1775–1817)
MANSFIELD PARK

A poor person who is unhappy is in a better position than a rich person who is unhappy. Because the poor person has hope. He thinks money will help.

JEAN KERR

Money won't make you happy . . . but everyone has to find out for themselves.

ZIG ZIGLAR

Save a little money each month and at the end of the year you'll be surprised at how little you have.

ERNEST HASKINGS

Money is flat and meant to be piled up.

SCOTTISH PROVERB

Money answereth all things.

ECCLESIASTIES 10:19

The fundamental evil of the world arose from the fact that the good Lord has not created money enough.

HEINRICH HEINE (1797–1856)

In suggesting gifts: Money is appropriate and one size fits all.

WILLIAM RANDOLPH HEARST

We are confronted with insurmountable opportunities.

POGO
WALT KELLY (1913–1973)

We make our fortunes and call them fate.

BENJAMIN DISRAELI (1804–1881)
QUOTED IN JAMES H. AUSTIN, *CHASE, CHANCE AND CREATIVITY*

It is the wretchedness of being rich that you have to live with rich people.

LOGAN PEARSALL SMITH (1865–1946)
AFTERTHOUGHTS

Abundance of money is a trial for a man.

MOROCCAN PROVERB

Money-getters are the benefactors of our race. To them
. . . are we indebted for institutions of learning, and of
art, our academies, colleges and churches.

P. T. Barnum (1810–1891)

Weapons are like money; no one knows the meaning of
enough.

Martin Amis

Making money is a hobby that will complement any
other hobbies you have beautifully.

Scott Alexander

Money is a kind of poetry.

WALLACE STEVENS

Nothing is more admirable than the fortitude with which millionaires tolerate the disadvantages of their wealth.

REX STOUT (1886–1975)
AUTHOR AND CREATOR OF THE NERO WOLFE DETECTIVE SERIES

Having money is rather like being a blond. It is more fun but not vital.

MARY QUANT

What is the chief end of Man?—to get rich. In what
way?—dishonestly if we can; honestly if we must.

MARK TWAIN
THE REVISED CATECHISM (1871)

Ill fares the land, to hastening ills a prey
Where wealth accumulates, and men decay

OLIVER GOLDSMITH (C.1728–1774)
THE DESERTED VILLAGE

Being rich ain't what it's cracked up to be. It's just worry and worry, and sweat and sweat, and a-wishing you was dead all the time.

MARK TWAIN
THE ADVENTURES OF TOM SAWYER

What is a man profited, if he shall gain the whole world, and lose his own soul?

MATTHEW 16:26

Wealth is not without its advantages and the case to the contrary, although it has often been made, has never proved widely persuasive.

JOHN KENNETH GALBRAITH
THE AFFLUENT SOCIETY (1958)

The ideas I stand for are not mine. I borrowed them from Socrates. I swiped them from Chesterfield. I stole them from Jesus. And I put them in a book. If you don't like their rules, whose would you use?

DALE CARNEGIE, FROM HIS BOOK *HOW TO WIN FRIENDS AND INFLUENCE PEOPLE*

It is ideas, not vested interests, which are dangerous for good or evil.

JOHN MAYNARD KEYNES (1883–1946)

Wealth is the product of industry, ambition, character and untiring effort.

CALVIN COOLIDGE (1872–1933)

A rich man told me recently that a liberal is a man who tells other people what to do with their money.

IMAMU AMIRI BARAKA

The only question with wealth is what you do with it.

JOHN D. ROCKEFELLER JR. (1874–1960)

Success is the one unpardonable sin against one's fellows.

AMBROSE BIERCE (1842–1914)

Those who condemn wealth are those who have none and see no chance of getting it.

WILLIAM PENN PATRICK

———————

Money is not the most important thing in the world. Love is. Fortunately, I love money.

JACKIE MASON

———————

Chance fights ever on the side of the prudent.

EURIPIDES (480–406 B.C.)

Luck never made a man wise.

SENECA (C. 4 B.C.–A.D. 65)
LETTERS TO LUCILIUS

How unfortunate and how narrowing a thing it is for a man to have wealth who makes a god of it instead of a servant.

MARK TWAIN (1835–1910)
OPEN LETTER TO COMMODORE VANDERBILT (1869)

In America, money takes the place of God.

ANZIA YEZIERSKA

People are smart, but they tend to make big errors, and they do it in groups.

ROBERT SHILLER
NEW YORK TIMES, APRIL 30, 2000

———•••••———

It has struck me that all men's misfortunes spring from the single cause that they are unable to stay quietly in one room.

LOUIS PASCAL

———•••••———

Buying options, futures, or commodities is not investing; it's gambling.

ERIC TYSON
MUTUAL FUNDS FOR DUMMIES (1998)

For *the kingdom of heaven is* as a man traveling into a far country who called his own servants, and delivered unto them his goods.

And unto one he gave five talents [a talent was 15 years' wages for a laborer], to another two, and to another one; to every man according to his several ability; and straightaway took his journey.

Then he that had received the five talents went and traded with the same, and made them other five talents.

And likewise he that had received two, he also gained other two.

But he that had received one went and digged in the earth, and hid his lord's money.

After a long time the lord of those servants cometh, and reckoneth with them.

And so he that had received five talents came and brought other five talents, saying, Lord, thou deliveredst unto me five talents: behold, I have gained beside them five talents more.

His lord said unto him, Well done, thou good and faithful servant: thou has been faithful over a few things, I will make thee ruler over many things: enter thou into the joy of thy lord.

He also that had received two talents came and said, Lord, thou deliveredst unto me two talents: behold, I have gained two other talents beside them.

His lord said unto him, Well done, good and faithful servant; thou has been faithful over a few things, I will make thee ruler over many things; enter thou in the joy of thy lord.

Then he which had received the one talent came and said, Lord, I knew thee that thou art an hard man, reaping where thou hast not sown, and gathering where thou has not strawed:

And I was afraid, and went and hid thy talent in the earth: lo, there thou hast that is thine.

His lord answered and said unto him, Thou wicked and slothful servant, thou knewest that I reap where I sowed not, and gather where I have not strawed:

Thou oughtest therefore to have put my money to the exchangers, and then at my coming I should have received mine own with usury.

Take therefore the talent from him, and give it unto him which hath ten talents.

For unto every one that hath shall be given, and he shall have abundance: but from him that hath not shall be taken away even that which he hath.

And cast ye the unprofitable servant into outer darkness: there shall be weeping and gnashing of teeth.

THE PARABLE OF THE TALENTS
MATTHEW 25:14–30 (KING JAMES VERSION)

Get inside information from the president and you will probably lose half of your money. If you get it from the chairman, you will lose all of it.

JIM ROGERS
INVESTMENT BIKER: ON THE ROAD WITH JIM ROGERS

———————

In business, the earning of profit is something more than an incident of success. It is an essential condition of success. It is an essential condition of success because the continued absence of profit itself spells failure.

JUSTICE LOUIS D. BRANDEIS (1856–1941)

———————

The only point in making money is you can tell some big shot where to go.

HUMPHREY BOGART

For stock speculation is largely a matter of A trying to decide what B, C and D are likely to think—with B, C and D trying to do the same.

BENJAMIN GRAHAM AND DAVID L. DODD
SECURITY ANALYSIS (1934)

———•••———

Billy Rose described the problem of overdiversification: "If you have a harem of forty women, you never get to know any of them very well."

WARREN BUFFETT
LETTER TO BERKSHIRE HATHAWAY INC. SHAREHOLDERS (1984)

"My other piece of advice, Copperfield, you know. Annual income twenty pounds, annual expenditure nineteen six, result happiness. Annual income twenty pounds, annual expenditure twenty pounds ought and six, result misery."

CHARLES DICKENS (1812–1870)
MR. MICAWBER IN DAVID COPPERFIELD (1849–1850)

———•••••———

Can anybody remember when the times were not hard and money not scarce?

RALPH WALDO EMERSON

I'm living so far beyond my income that we may almost be said to be living apart.

EE CUMMINGS (1894–1962)

Those who have some means think that the most important thing in the world is love. The poor know it is money.

GERALD BRENNAN

We must keep in mind that the stock market is a manifestation of our desire to be productive and contribute to our families and communities.

TAD CRAWFORD
FOREWORD TO JOHN BROOKS'S ONCE IN GOLCONDA (1997)

After all, the chief business of the American people is business. They are profoundly concerned with producing, buying, selling, investing and prospering in the world.

CALVIN COOLIDGE (1872–1933)

Business? It's quite simple: it's other people's money.

ALEXANDER DUMAS
LA QUESTION D'ARGENT

Money never remains just coins and pieces of paper. Money can be translated into the beauty of living, a support of misfortune, an education, or future security. It also can be translated into a source of bitterness.

SYLVIA PORTER (1913–1991)

There are two times in a man's life when he should not speculate: when he can't afford it and when he can.

MARK TWAIN

Never invest your money in anything that eats or needs repainting.

BILLY ROSE (1899–1966)

No man's credit is as good as his money.

ED HOWE

Don't try to buy at the bottom and sell at the top. It can't be done except by liars.

BERNARD BARUCH (1870–1965)

They use [how much] money they've spent as a measure of success because there's very little else to measure.

DAVID BRINKLEY

Buy an annuity cheap, and make your life interesting to yourself and everybody else that watches the speculation.

CHARLES DICKENS
MARTIN CHUZZLEWIT (1843–1844)

———•••——

I made my money by selling too soon.

BERNARD BARUCH (1870–1965)

To turn $100 into $110 is work. To turn $100 million into $110 million is inevitable.

EDGAR BRONFMAN, CHAIRMAN, SEAGRAM CO.
NEWSWEEK, DECEMBER 2, 1985

It's always too early to quit.

NORMAN VINCENT PEALE (1898–1993)

Emotions are your worst enemy in the stock market.

DON HAYS, RETIRED MARKET STRATEGIST

Men in the uniform of Wall Street retirement: black Chesterfield coat, rimless glasses and the *Times* folded to the obituary page.

JIMMY BRESLIN

———•+•+•———

When you sell in desperation, you always sell cheap.

PETER LYNCH
ONE UP ON WALL STREET

I don't much believe in stocks. I never buy industrials. Railroads and real estate are the things I like. There's no great secret in fortune-making. All you have to do is buy cheap and sell dear, act with thrift and shrewdness and be persistent.

HETTY GREEN, "THE WITCH OF WALL STREET," FIRST WOMAN
KNOWN TO HAVE MADE A FORTUNE ON WALL STREET
FROM BOYDEN SPARKES AND SAMUEL TAYLOR MOORE'S
THE WITCH OF WALL STREET: HETTY GREEN (1935)

I had no ambition to make a fortune. Mere money-making has never been my goal. I had an ambition to build.

JOHN D. ROCKEFELLER, JR. (1874–1960)

Be not made a beggar by banqueting upon borrowing.

THE APOCHRYPHA

If you would know the value of money, go and borrow some.

BENJAMIN FRANKLIN (1706–1790)

The borrower is servant to the lender.

PROVERBS 22:7

A nation is not in danger of financial disaster merely because it owes itself money.

ANDREW MELLON

Borrowed thoughts, like borrowed money, only show the poverty of the borrower.

LADY MARGUERITE BLESSINGTON

Take what you want, said God, take it—and pay for it.

SPANISH PROVERB

Solvency is maintained by means of a national debt on the principle, "If you will not lend me the money, how can I pay you?"

RALPH WALDO EMERSON

Knowing about markets is knowing about people's weaknesses.

MICHAEL LEWIS
LIAR'S POKER (1990)

In investing money, the amount of investment you want should depend on whether you want to eat well or sleep well.

J. KENNFIELD MORLEY

Like the Stock Market, Only Faster

OFF-TRACK BETTING BILLBOARD IN CONNECTICUT
FROM ROBERT J. SHILLER'S *IRRATIONAL EXUBERANCE* (2000)

———•••———

Blessed is the man who expects nothing, for he shall never be disappointed.

ALEXANDER POPE (1688–1744)
LETTER TO FORTESCUE

———•••———

How the market reacts to bad news is more important than the news itself.

ANONYMOUS WALL STREET SAYING

The chief losses to investors come from the purchase of low-quality securities at times of favorable business conditions.

BENJAMIN GRAHAM

I don't know what the seven wonders of the world are, but I do know the eighth—compound interest.

BARON ROTHSCHILD

The Rule of 72 determines how long it will take to double your money—divide the rate of return into 72.

INVESTMENT RULE OF THUMB

The safe way to double your money is to fold it over once and put it in your pocket.

ELBERT "KIN" HUBBARD (1856–1915)

Great companies bought at great prices should be like great friends—you don't drop them precipitously.

SHELBY DAVIS

Nothing is so strongly fortified that it cannot be taken by money.

MARCUS CICERO (106–43 B.C.)

Take windfall profits when you have them.

ANONYMOUS WALL STREET ADAGE

Over the long term, low price/earnings ratio stocks will outperform high P/E stocks.

WALL STREET ADAGE

Stocks always seem to rise on the day before a holiday—any holiday.

WALL STREET ADAGE

———•••••———

January tends to set the tone for the rest of the market year.

WALL STREET ADAGE

———•••••———

A loss never bothers me after I take it. I forget it. But being wrong—taking the loss—that is what does damage to the pocketbook and to the soul.

JESSE LIVERMORE, LEGENDARY TRADER,
AFTER THE 1929 CRASH

October. This is one of the peculiarly dangerous months to speculate in stocks. The others are July, January, September, April, November, May, March, June, December, August and February.

MARK TWAIN

As a bull market begins to peak, sell the stock that has gone up the most—it will drop the fastest. Sell the stock that has gone up the *least*—it didn't go up, so it must go down.

ANONYMOUS WALL STREET ADAGE

Only buy something that you'd be perfectly happy to hold if the market shut down for 10 years.

WARREN BUFFETT

A rising tide raises all ships.

ANONYMOUS WALL STREET ADAGE

The hard-to-accept great paradox in the stock market is that what seems too high and risky to the majority usually goes higher and what seems low and cheap usually goes lower.

WILLIAM O'NEIL
FOUNDER OF *INVESTOR'S BUSINESS DAILY*

My biggest winners continue to be stocks I've held for three and even four years.

PETER LYNCH

The intelligent investor is likely to need considerable willpower to keep from following the crowd.

BENJAMIN GRAHAM (1896–1976)

Don't buck the trend, your trade won't be the one that turns the market around.

WALL STREET ADAGE

Time is the friend of stocks; the enemy of bonds.

WALL STREET ADAGE

The worse you feel, usually because the news is bad, the safer the market is. The better you feel, usually because the news is good, the closer you are to a top.

JOHN TRAIN, AUTHOR AND HEAD OF TRAIN, SMITH INVESTMENT COUNSEL, NEW YORK

Never buy a stock that won't go *up* in a bull market. Never sell a stock that won't go *down* in a bear market.

WALL STREET ADAGE

———•••———

If the job has been correctly done when a common stock is purchased, the time to sell it is almost never.

PHILIP FISCHER, WRITER-INVESTOR

———•••———

Most investors also seem to view the stock market as a force of nature unto itself. They do not fully realize that they themselves, as a group, determine the level of the market.

ROBERT J. SHILLER
IRRATIONAL EXUBERANCE (2000)

Low inflation and low interest rates usually result in a strong stock market.

WALL STREET ADAGE

———•••—

Even those with a disciplined long-term approach like ours have to sit back and say "wow."

FULL-PAGE MERRILL LYNCH AD, WHEN THE DOW JONES INDUSTRIAL AVERAGE FIRST SURPASSED 10,000 IN MARCH 1999

———•••—

[E]ven when the underlying motive of purchase is mere speculative greed, human nature desires to conceal this unlovely impulse behind a screen of apparent logic and good sense.

BENJAMIN GRAHAM AND DAVID DODD
SECURITY ANALYSIS (1934)

The shortest recorded period of time lies between the minute you put some money away for a rainy day and the unexpected arrival of rain.

JANE BRYANT QUINN

The love of money as a possession—as distinguished from the love of money as a means to the enjoyments and realities of life—will be recognized for what it is, a somewhat disgusting morbidity, one of those semi-criminal, semi-pathological propensities which one hands over with a shudder to the specialists in mental disease.

JOHN MAYNARD KEYNES, 1931

It's a terribly hard job to spend a billion dollars and get your money's worth.

GEORGE M. HUMPHREY, FORMER U.S. SECRETARY OF THE TREASURY

The only thing money gives you is the freedom of not worrying about money.

JOHNNY CARSON

It doesn't matter if you're rich or poor—as long as you've got money.

JOE E. LEWIS

How is the stock market like a river with an average depth of one foot?

The average doesn't tell you about deep holes in which the unsuspecting drown.

ANONYMOUS WALL STREET RIDDLE

Most people will say [they invest] "to make money" and that's wrong. You invest to satisfy goals.

MARSHALL E. BLUME, WHARTON SCHOOL FINANCE PROFESSOR
QUOTED IN THE *PHILADELPHIA INQUIRER*, OCTOBER 10, 1999

You have to decide whether you want to make money or make sense, because the two are mutually exclusive.

RICHARD FULLER (1895–1983)

Fools and greed usually go hand in hand, which creates a field of opportunity for the rational man.

MARY BUFFETT AND DAVID CLARK
BUFFETTOLOGY (1999)

Children are rarely in the position to lend one a truly interesting sum of money. There are, however, exceptions, and such children are an excellent addition to any party.

FRAN LEBOWITZ

All money is a matter of belief.

ADAM SMITH

⸻ ❖ ⸻

Rule Number One: Never Lose Money. Rule Number Two: Never Forget Rule Number One.

WARREN BUFFETT

6

The Blessed, Cursed Fed

[The seven-member Federal Reserve Board of Governors decides] the largest questions of the political economy, including who shall prosper and who shall fail.

WILLIAM GREIDER, *SECRETS OF THE TEMPLE*

———————

I think the Fed is going to win the battle against inflation—and it may be at the expense of the stock market.

WILLIAM STEVENS, PRINCIPAL, MONTGOMERY ASSET MANAGEMENT
WALL STREET JOURNAL, MAY 19, 2000

He is a dream wrecker, that Greenspan. He wants us all to work at McDonald's until we are 72.

HENRY JOHNSEN, RETIRED PROFESSOR
FROM LANDON THOMAS JR.'S,"BRING ME THE HEAD
OF ALAN GREENSPAN," *SMARTMONEY*, AUGUST 2000

———◆◆◆———

A clarinet player who fell in love with economics, an economist who fell in love with politics, [Greenspan] is something of an enigma.

STEVEN K. BECKNER
BACK FROM THE BRINK: THE GREENSPAN YEARS

As an answer to the great [financial] panics [in the twentieth century] the [Federal Reserve] System was notably defective.

JOHN KENNETH GALBRAITH
MONEY, WHENCE IT CAME, WHERE IT WENT (1975)

———•••———

The economy we see today is to a substantial extent a result of what Paul [Volcker] and his colleagues were able to do with the extraordinary inflationary acceleration, which had it not been reined in, the issue we'd be talking about today would [be] . . . the stability of our society.

ALAN GREENSPAN, ON HIS PREDECESSOR AS FED CHAIRMAN
FROM STEVEN BECKNER'S *BACK FROM THE BRINK:
THE GREENSPAN YEARS*

What's the subject of life—to get rich? All of those fellows out there getting rich could be dancing around the real subject of life.

PAUL VOLCKER, FORMER CHAIRMAN, FEDERAL RESERVE SYSTEM

———•••••———

The Federal Reserve System is treated by nearly all economists with reverence. . . . It makes many mistakes but these are always interesting errors of judgment. They are examined not critically but respectfully to discover why men of insight went wrong.

JOHN KENNETH GALBRAITH
MONEY, WHENCE IT CAME, WHERE IT WENT (1975)

[S]ince many in Washington did not truly grasp Wall Street's function in the American System, they could not understand the Federal Reserve's either.

WILLIAM GREIDER
SECRETS OF THE TEMPLE: HOW THE FEDERAL RESERVE RUNS THE COUNTRY (1989)

The Washington reflex: you discover a problem, throw money at it and hope somehow that it will go away.

KENNETH KEATING

A modern version of the prophets who spoke in riddles, Greenspan likes to pose questions rather than make pronouncements. In the public exegesis of his remarks, it is often forgotten that, when it comes to such questions, even he does not know the answers.

ROBERT J. SHILLER
IRRATIONAL EXUBERANCE (2000)

Rivlin: Do you really want to say that?
Greenspan: I think I do.

EXCHANGE BETWEEN ALICE RIVLIN, THEN FED VICE CHAIRMAN, AND CHAIRMAN GREENSPAN ABOUT HIS INTENTION TO SAY HIGH STOCK PRICES MIGHT BE DUE TO "IRRATIONAL EXUBERANCE" IN A SPEECH HE PLANNED TO MAKE ON DECEMBER 5, 1996
WALL STREET JOURNAL, MAY 8, 2000

I wish I could say that there is a bound volume of immutable instructions on my desk on how effectively to implement policy to achieve our goals of maximum employment, sustainable economic growth, and price stability.

FED CHAIRMAN ALAN GREENSPAN
AT THE AMERICAN ENTERPRISE INSTITUTE
ANNUAL DINNER, DECEMBER 5, 1996

———•◦•◦•———

I am very careful about bringing people into my confidence. I want to see the color of their eyes.

E. GERALD CORRIGAN, ON BECOMING PRESIDENT
OF THE FEDERAL RESERVE BANK IN MINNEAPOLIS

Just as the financial press watches the Fed, the Fed watches the financial press, much more than people imagine. A lot of our analysis of markets actually comes from the press.

ANONYMOUS FED RESEARCH ECONOMIST
QUOTED IN WILLIAM GRIEDER'S SECRETS OF THE TEMPLE (1989)

7

*Experts
(So Called)*

Wall Street analysts are known to have a lot of habits endemic to the breed. One is a tendency toward insisting that most of the stocks they follow will beat the market—an assertion on a par with the claim that all children in Lake Wobegon are above average.

MICHAEL SANTOLI
BARRON'S, MAY 15, 2000

[H]e's your salesman to investors.

INFOSPACE CHAIRMAN NAVEEN JAIN
ON AN ANALYST'S IMPORTANCE TO A PUBLIC COMPANY
WALL STREET JOURNAL, JULY 14, 2000

That much of what was repeated about the market—then as now—bore no relation to reality is important, but not remarkable.

JOHN KENNETH GALBRAITH
THE GREAT CRASH OF 1929 (1954 EDITION)

Prophecy is the most gratuitous form of error.

GEORGE ELIOT (1819–1880)
[PSEUDONYM OF MARIAN EVANS CROSS]
MIDDLEMARCH

Isn't it strange? The same people who laugh at gypsy fortune tellers take economists seriously.

CINCINNATI ENQUIRER

Ask five economists and you'll get five different answers (six if one went to Harvard).

EDGAR FIEDLER, FORMER CHIEF ECONOMIST AT THE CONFERENCE BOARD, "THE THREE Rs OF ECONOMIC FORECASTING— IRRATIONAL, IRRELEVANT AND IRREVERENT" *ACROSS THE BOARD* MAGAZINE, AUGUST 1977

An economist is an expert who will know tomorrow why the things he predicted yesterday didn't happen today.

LAURENCE J. PETER, AUTHOR ASSOCIATED MOST FAMOUSLY WITH THE PETER PRINCIPLE

Harry Truman once said he wanted a one-armed economist who didn't always say, "On the other hand."

JOHN KENNETH GALBRAITH
LOS ANGELES TIMES, DECEMBER 12, 2000

When better business decisions are made, economists won't make them.

H. V. PROCHNOW, AUTHOR, HUMORIST

Business is like sex. When it's good, it's very, very good; when it's not so good, it's still good.

GEORGE KATONA, UNIVERSITY OF MICHIGAN BUSINESS SURVEY RESEARCH BUREAU

Ye know not what shall be on the morrow.

JAMES 4:14

———•••———

As some perceptive person once said, if all the economists of the world were laid end to end, it wouldn't be a bad thing.

PETER LYNCH
ONE UP ON WALL STREET

———•••———

You know what the difference is between a dead skunk and a dead banker on the road? There's skid marks by the skunk.

ANONYMOUS

If economists were any good at business, they would be rich men instead of advisers to rich men.

KIRK KERKORIAN
QUOTED IN ROBERT KENT'S *MONEY TALKS* (1985)

What we anticipate seldom occurs: what we least expected generally happens.

BENJAMIN DISRAELI (1804–1881)
HENRIETTA TEMPLE (1837)

Economics is extremely useful as a form of employment for economists.

JOHN KENNETH GALBRAITH

An expert is someone who knows more and more about less and less, until eventually he knows everything about nothing.

ANONYMOUS

Economic forecasts are wrong a large part of the time.

L. DOUGLAS LEE, CHIEF ECONOMIST, HSBC SECURITIES
NEW YORK TIMES, FEBRUARY 7, 1999

The trouble with the world is that the stupid are cock-sure and the intelligent are full of doubt.

BERTRAND RUSSELL (1872–1970)

Wisdom, itself, is often an abstraction associated not with fact or reality but with the man who asserts it and the manner of its assertion.

JOHN KENNETH GALBRAITH
THE GREAT CRASH OF 1929 (1954 EDITION)

A smattering of everything, and a knowledge of nothing.

CHARLES DICKENS (1812–1870)
SKETCHES BY BOZ (1836–1837)

Entrepreneurs are risk takers, willing to roll the dice with their money or reputations on the line in support of an idea or an enterprise. They willingly assume responsibility for the success or failure of a venture and are answerable for all its facets.

VICTOR KIAM

———•••——

Even if [your] business fails, it can only be a great learning experience. . . . But then it is harder to take that advice than to give it. After all, I'm a tenured professor.

WILLIAM A. SAHLMAN, HARVARD BUSINESS SCHOOL'S
ENTREPRENEURIAL STUDIES PROGRAM
NEW YORK TIMES, APRIL 17, 2000

I find it rather easy to portray a businessman. Being bland, rather cruel and incompetent comes naturally to me.

JOHN CLEESE

Some extremely sharp investment advisors can get you in at the bottom of the market. Some extremely sharp ones can get you out at the top. They are never the same people.

GARY NORTH, DOOMSAYER, PUBLISHER
OF THE NEWSLETTER *REMNANT REVIEW*

Forget technical analysis. It is not knowable from what a stock did last month or last year, how it will do next month or next year.

JOHN TRAIN

———

Incomprehensible jargon is the hallmark of a profession.

KINGMAN BREWSTER, U.S. AMBASSADOR TO BRITAIN

———

Back in graduate school I learned the market goes up nine percent a year, and since then it's never gone up nine percent in a year. . . .

PETER LYNCH

The trouble with our times is that the future is not what it used to be.

PAUL VALERY (1871–1945)

———•◦•◦•———

Needless to say, the analyst cannot be right all the time. Furthermore, a conclusion may be logically right but work out badly in practice.

BENJAMIN GRAHAM AND DAVID DODD
SECURITY ANALYSIS (1934)

They usually say: "Oh my God, I thought you were older."

> JUSTIN HENDRIX, 19, WHO POSTS HIS STOCK ADVICE
> ON IEXCHANGE.COM AS "DR. WALL STREET";
> THE WEB SITE RANKED HIM IN THE TOP 15 OF ITS
> MORE THAN 8,000 ANALYSTS
> *WALL STREET JOURNAL,* JULY 10, 2000

Prediction is very difficult, especially about the future.

> NIELS BOHR (1885–1962)

8

When the Dow Breaks

One can relish the varied idiocy of human action during
a panic to the full, for, while it is a time of great tragedy,
nothing is being lost but money.

JOHN KENNENTH GALBRAITH
THE GREAT CRASH OF 1929 (1954 EDITION)

After a storm comes a calm.

MATTHEW HENRY (1662–1714)
COMMENTARIES

We face a far greater risk of psychological depression than of economic recession.

TODD G. BUCHHOLZ
WALL STREET JOURNAL EDITORIAL PAGE, APRIL 12, 2000

It was seen that somebody must lose fearfully in the end. As this conviction spread, prices fell, and never rose again. Confidence was destroyed, and a universal panic seized up the [tulip] dealers. . . . Hundreds who, a few months previously, had begun to doubt that there was such a thing as poverty in the land suddenly found themselves the possessors of a few bulbs, which nobody would buy. . . .

CHARLES MACKAY
EXTRAORDINARY POPULAR DELUSIONS
& THE MADNESS OF CROWDS (1852)

Sell 'em all! They're not worth anything.

BEN "SELL 'EM BEN" SMITH,
WHO MADE A FORTUNE SELLING SHORT IN 1929
FROM JOHN BROOKS'S *ONCE IN GOLCONDA*

The repeated demonstration, which the market has given of its ability to come back with renewed strength after a sharp reaction, has engendered a spirit of indifference.

THE *NEW YORK TIMES*, TWO DAYS BEFORE
THE 1929 MARKET CRASH

In adversity assume the countenance of prosperity, and in prosperity moderate the temper and desires.

TITUS LIVIUS (59 B.C.–A.D. 17)

Fortune is not satisfied with inflicting one calamity.

PUBLILIUS SYRUS (FIRST CENTURY B.C.)
MAXIM 274

There is something in the wind.

SHAKESPEARE
THE COMEDY OF ERRORS, ACT III, SCENE I, LINE 69

There was a time when a fool and his money were soon parted, but now it happens to everybody.

ADLAI STEVENSON (1900–1965)

When stock prices are rising, it's called "momentum investing"; when they are falling, it's called "panic."

PAUL KRUGMAN, ECONOMIST AND AUTHOR

Losing potential profits hurts the ego; losing money really hurts.

GERALD APPEL, PRESIDENT, SIGNALERT, AN INVESTMENT MANAGEMENT FIRM

Whatever you can lose, you should reckon of no account.

PUBLILIUS SYRUS (FIRST CENTURY B.C.)
MAXIM 191

The word "crisis" in Chinese is composed of two characters: the first, the symbol of danger; the second, opportunity.

ANONYMOUS

In times like these, it helps to recall that there have always been times like these.

PAUL HARVEY, RADIO COMMENTATOR AND NEWSCASTER

If you suffer, thank God!—it is a sure sign that you are alive.

ELBERT "KIN" HUBBARD (1856–1915)

That which does not kill us makes us stronger.

FRIEDRICH NIETZSCHE (1844–1900)

Everything is funny as long as it is happening to somebody else.

WILL ROGERS (1879–1935)

I am not ashamed to record that in those days I felt and said I would be willing to part with half of what I had if I could be sure of keeping, under law and order, the other half.

JOSEPH KENNEDY, COMMENTING ON THE GREAT DEPRESSION

To speak out against madness may be to ruin those who have succumbed to it. So the wise of Wall Street are nearly always silent. The foolish thus have the field to themselves. None rebukes them.

JOHN KENNETH GALBRAITH
THE GREAT CRASH OF 1929 (1954 EDITION)

———

There are crimes far worse than murder for which men should be reviled and punished.

HERBERT HOOVER
THE GREAT DEPRESSION, 1929–1941 (1952)

———

A time to get, and a time to lose.

ECCLESIASTES 3:6

If buying and selling stocks is wrong, the government should close the stock exchange. If not, the Federal Reserve should mind its own business.

ARTHUR BRISBANE, COLUMNIST FOR HEARST NEWSPAPERS,
ON FED EFFORTS TO RESTRAIN MARGIN BUYING DURING '29 PANIC

Pain and foolishness lead to great bliss and complete knowledge, for Eternal Wisdom created nothing under the sun in vain.

KAHLIL GIBRAN (1883–1931)
THE VOICE OF THE POET

Above all, it's evident that the capacity of the financial community for ignoring evidence of accumulating trouble, even of wishing devoutly that it go unmentioned, is as great as ever.

JOHN KENNETH GALBRAITH
INTRODUCTION TO *THE GREAT CRASH OF 1929* (1961 EDITION)

[The] investor who purchases securities at this time with the discrimination that as always is a condition of prudent investing may do so with utmost confidence.

EDITORIAL PUBLISHED IN THE *NEW YORK TIMES* THE MORNING OF
TUESDAY, OCTOBER 29, 1929, LATER KNOWN AS BLACK TUESDAY

Fear is the darkroom where negatives are developed.

MICHAEL PRITCHARD, WRITER, MOTIVATIONAL SPEAKER,
FORMER STAND-UP COMEDIAN

———•••———

The worse a situation becomes, the less it takes to turn it around—and the bigger the upside.

GEORGE SOROS, FAMED HEDGE FUND OPERATOR

I'm quite fond of 1929. My dad was a stock salesman at the time, and after the Crash came . . . he was afraid to call anyone . . . so he just stayed home in the afternoons. And there wasn't television then. Soooo . . . I was conceived on or about November 30, 1929 . . . and I've forever had a kind of warm feeling about the Crash.

"MR. BUFFETT ON THE STOCK MARKET"
CAROL LOOMIS WITH EDITING BY WARREN BUFFETT,
FORTUNE (NOVEMBER 22, 1999)

———•••———

Far more money has been lost by investors preparing for corrections or trying to anticipate corrections than has been lost in corrections themselves.

PETER LYNCH

The time to buy securities is when the media is so full of doom that your trembling hand can scarcely hold the telephone to call your broker with a buy order.

JAMES MICHAELS, EDITOR EMERITUS, *FORBES* MAGAZINE

Try to think about it as Charles Darwin meeting Adam Smith.

GARY RIESCHEL, PARTNER WITH SOFTBANK TECHNOLOGY PARTNERS, ON COLLAPSE OF TECH STOCKS
NEW YORK TIMES, APRIL 23, 2000

To be a successful market timer you would have to be right twice, when you buy and when you sell. To be right the first time, you have a 50 percent chance—to be right on both sides of the trade, you have a 15 percent chance.

ANONYMOUS

———•⊷••⊶•———

It was the steady investors who kept their heads when the stock market tanked in October 1987, and then saw the value of their holdings eventually recover and continue to produce attractive returns.

BURTON MALKIEL, PRINCETON PROFESSOR OF FINANCE

Never before has American business been as firmly entrenched for prosperity as it is today. . . . Stocks may go up and stocks may go down, but the nation will prosper.

CHARLES SCHWAB, DECEMBER 10, 1929
FROM JOHN BROOKS'S *ONCE IN GOLCONDA*

Our banking system grew by accident; and whenever something happens by accident, it becomes a religion.

WALTER WRISTON
BUSINESS WEEK, JANUARY 20, 1975

A bank is a place that will lend you money if you can prove you don't need it.

BOB HOPE

———

I never gamble.

COMMENT TO BERNARD BARUCH BY JOHN PIERPONT MORGAN, WHOSE J. P. MORGAN INVESTMENT BANK SUFFERED THE LEAST OF ALL WALL STREET BANKS IN THE '29 CRASH
FROM RON CHERNOW'S *THE HOUSE OF MORGAN* (1991)

9

Scams and Scoundrels

It was a maxim with Foxey—our revered father, gentle-men—"Always suspect everybody."

CHARLES DICKENS
THE OLD CURIOSITY SHOP (1841)

———◆◆◆———

I trade with the boys and skin 'em and I just beat 'em every time I can. I want to make 'em sharp.

WILLIAM AVERY ROCKEFELLER,
FATHER OF JOHN D. ROCKEFELLER, SR.

It's them that takes advantage that get advantage i' this world.

GEORGE ELIOT (1819–1880)
ADAM BEDE (1859)

The secret of great fortunes with no apparent source is a forgotten crime, forgotten because it was properly carried out.

HONORÉ DE BALZAC (1799–1850)
OLD GORIOT (1834)

Half the world is composed of idiots, the other half of people clever enough to take indecent advantage of them.

WALTER KERR, THEATER CRITIC AND AUTHOR (1913–1996)

We all need money, but there are degrees of desperation.

ANTHONY BURGESS (1917–1993)

A man is usually more careful of his money than he is of his principles.

EDGAR WATSON HOWE (1853–1937)

Don't steal; thoul't never thus compete successfully in business. Cheat.

AMBROSE BIERCE (1842–C. 1914)

No one in this world, so far as I know . . . has ever lost money by underestimating the intelligence of the great masses of the plain people.

H. L. MENCKEN (1880–1956)
"NOTES ON JOURNALISM"
CHICAGO TRIBUNE, SEPTEMBER 19, 1926

We must scrunch or be scrunched.

CHARLES DICKENS (1812–1870)
OUR MUTUAL FRIEND

When you go to buy, use your eyes, not your ears.

CZECH PROVERB

Honesty pays, but it doesn't seem to pay enough to suit some people.

FRANK MCKINNEY "KIN" HUBBARD (1868–1930)

The secret of life is honesty and fair dealing. If you can fake that, you've got it made.

GROUCHO MARX (1895–1977)

He that resolves to deal with none but honest men must leave off dealing.

THOMAS FULLER (1654–1734)
GNOMOLOGIA (1732)

To be honest, as this world goes, is to be one man picked out of ten thousand.

WILLIAM SHAKESPEARE (1564–1616)
HAMLET

It is difficult but not impossible to conduct strictly honest business. What is true is that honesty is incompatible with amassing of a large fortune.

MOHANDAS K. GANDHI (1869–1948)

Make money by fair means if you can; if not, by any means make money.

HORACE (65–68 B.C.)
EPISTLES, BOOK I

Greed is all right. Greed is healthy. You can be greedy and still feel good about yourself.

IVAN BOESKY, COMMENCEMENT ADDRESS
AT BERKELEY, CALIF., MAY 18, 1986
MADE PRIOR TO HIS CONVICTION FOR INSIDER TRADING

A single bag of money is stronger than two bags of truth.

DANISH PROVERB

The modern conservative is engaged in one of man's oldest exercises in moral philosophy; that is, the search for a superior moral justification for selfishness.

JOHN KENNETH GALBRAITH

He that maketh haste to be rich shall not be innocent.

PROVERBS 28:20

The rich man . . . is always sold to the institution which makes him rich. Absolutely speaking, the more money, the less virtue.

HENRY DAVID THOREAU

No man should be in public office who can't make more money in private life.

THOMAS DEWEY (1902–1971)

Look, we trade every day out there with hustlers, deal makers, shysters, con men . . . that's the way businesses get started. That's the way this country was built.

HERBERT ALLEN

I am still looking for the modern equivalent of those Quakers who ran successful businesses, made money because they offered honest products and treated their people decently. . . . This business creed, sadly, seems long forgotten.

ANITA RODDICK, BUSINESSWOMAN

[A] lie which is half a truth is ever the blackest of lies.

ALFRED, LORD TENNYSON (1809–1892)
SEA DREAMS

Promise, large promise, is the soul of advertisement.

SAMUEL JOHNSON (1709–1784)

———•••••———

I think that American salesmanship can be a weapon more powerful than the atomic bomb.

HENRY J. KAISER (1882–1967)

———•••••———

Let advertisers spend the same amount of money improving their product that they do on advertising and they wouldn't have to advertise it.

WILL ROGERS (1879–1935)

I've been reminding financial professionals to tell the truth, the whole truth and nothing but the truth.

LYNN E. TURNER, CHIEF ACCOUNTANT,
THE SECURITIES AND EXCHANGE COMMISSION
NEW YORK TIMES, MAY 14, 2000

Do other men for they would do you.

CHARLES DICKENS (1812–1870)
BARNABY RUDGE

I've learned that you never ask a tire salesman if you need new tires.

ANONYMOUS

Any scam artist that doesn't use the Internet ought to be sued for malpractice.

JOSEPH BORG, ALABAMA'S SECURITIES COMMISSIONER
WALL STREET JOURNAL, JUNE 22, 2000

———•••———

We must have a political state powerful enough to deal with corporate wealth, but how are we going to keep that state with its augmenting power from being captured by the force we want it to control?

VERNON LOUIS PARRINGTON (1871–1929)
PULITZER PRIZE–WINNING HISTORIAN

———•••———

I've been nitpicked to pieces by the goddamn bureaucracy.

TRAVIS REED

The only thing that saves us from the bureaucracy is its inefficiency.

SENATOR EUGENE MCCARTHY (1916–)

———◆◆◆◆———

The business of government is to keep the government out of business—that is, unless business needs government aid.

WILL ROGERS (1879–1935)

———◆◆◆◆———

Some see private enterprise as a predatory target to be shot, others as a cow to be milked, but few are those who see it as a sturdy horse pulling the wagon.

WINSTON CHURCHILL (1874–1965)

A great deal of the so-called government encroachment in the area of business, labor, and the professions has been asked for by the people misusing their freedom.

J. IRWIN MILLER, FORMER CHAIRMAN OF CUMMINS ENGINE COMPANY

The law's made to take care o'raskills.

GEORGE ELIOT (1819–1880)
THE MILL ON THE FLOSS

"If the law supposes that," said Mr. Bumble . . . "the law is a ass, a idiot."

CHARLES DICKENS (1812–1870)
OLIVER TWIST

[I]n shaping the laws that now govern Wall Street . . . virtually no aid or cooperation came from the denizens of that great marketplace we euphemistically call Wall Street. Indeed they were passed in the face of the bitter and powerfully organized opposition of the financial community.

FERDINAND PECORA, LEGAL COUNSEL TO SENATE PANEL
INVESTIGATING WALL STREET FOLLOWING THE 1929 CRASH
FROM MICHAEL LEWIS'S *THE MONEY CULTURE* (1991)

Those old Wall Street boys are putting up an awful fight to keep the government from putting a cop on their corner.

WILL ROGERS

The SEC is a force for good. But too often it's at the wrong place at the wrong time, swatting at flies while the big fish keep swimming along.

ALAN LECHNER
*STREET GAMES: INSIDE STORIES
OF THE WALL STREET HUSTLE* (1980)

POWER, n: The only narcotic regulated by the SEC instead of the FDA.

ANONYMOUS

People who think money can do anything may very well be suspected of doing anything for money.

MARY POOLE

It is the duty of government to make it difficult for people to do wrong, easy to do right.

WILLIAM E. GLADSTONE (1809–1898)

———•••••———

A prospectus is not designed to help investors, it is designed to disclose legal requirements.

A. MICHAEL LIPPER, FOUNDER OF LIPPER INC., A MUTUAL-FUND PERFORMANCE FIRM

———•••••———

The world wants to be deceived.

SEBASTIAN BRANT (C. 1458–1521)
THE SHIP OF FOOLS

But the most absurd and preposterous of all [stock companies whose stock was being bought in London in the early 1700s], and which shewed, more completely than any other, the utter madness of the people, was one started by an unknown adventurer, entitled, "*A company for carrying on an undertaking of great advantage, but nobody to know what it is.*"

CHARLES MACKAY
*EXTRAORDINARY POPULAR DELUSIONS
& THE MADNESS OF CROWDS* (1852)

But when to mischief mortals bend their will,
How soon they find fit instruments of ill!

ALEXANDER POPE (1688–1744)
THE RAPE OF THE LOCK

Show me a liar, and I'll show thee a thief.

GEORGE HERBERT (1593–1633)
JACULA PRUDENTUM

Every fortune ever made in finance has rested on a simple premise. Those with the most information make the most money. That edge, knowing what others don't, is priceless.

PAUL GIBSON
BEAR TRAP (1993)

Oh, what a tangled web we weave,
When first we practice to deceive!

SIR WALTER SCOTT (1771–1832)
MARMION (1808)

Skeptics are never deceived.

FRENCH PROVERB

— • — • — • —

... [I]t is always we who deceive ourselves.

JEAN JACQUES ROUSSEAU (1712–1778)
DISCOURSE UPON THE ORIGIN AND FOUNDATION
OF THE INEQUALITY AMONG MANKIND (1754)

— • — • — • —

Can you teach the crab to walk straight? You cannot.

ARISTOPHANES (C. 450–385 B.C.)
THE PEACE (C. 425 B.C.)

Many commit the same crimes with a very different result. One bears a cross for his crime; another a crown.

JUVENAL (C. 55–130)
SATIRES

Believe nothing and be on your guard against everything.

LATIN PROVERB

Great blunders are often made, like large ropes, of a multitude of fibers.

VICTOR HUGO (1802–1885)
LES MISERABLES (1862)

The nature of business is swindling.

AUGUST BEBEL (1840–1913)
COFOUNDER OF SOCIALIST WORKERS' PARTY IN GERMANY

Fortune favors the audacious.

DESIDERIUS ERASMUS (C. 1466–1536)

Jesus Saves. Satan Invests.

ANONYMOUS

The savings of many in the hands of one.

EUGENE V. DEBS (1855–1926)
ON WEALTH

———●•••●———

The purchase made, the fruits are to ensue: that profit's yet to come 'tween me and you.

WILLIAM SHAKESPEARE
OTHELLO, ACT II, SCENE 3

———●•••●———

FINANCE, n. The art or science of managing revenues and resources for the best advantage of the manager.

AMBROSE BIERCE (1842–1914)
THE DEVIL'S DICTIONARY

Behold the fool saith, "Put not all thine eggs in one basket"—which is but a manner of saying, "Scatter your money and your attention"; but the wise man saith, "Put all your eggs in one basket and—WATCH THAT BASKET."

MARK TWAIN
PUDD'N HEAD WILSON

I greatly fear my money is not safe.

WILLIAM SHAKESPEARE
THE COMEDY OF ERRORS

[H]ow little security have we when we trust our happiness in the hands of others!

WILLIAM HAZLITT (1778–1830)
TABLE TALK 1821–1822: ON LIVING TO ONE'S SELF

———◦•••◦———

Real knowledge is to know the extent of one's ignorance.

CONFUCIUS (551–479 B.C.)

———◦•••◦———

Get nervous if a planner or adviser spends time bragging about the investment returns of his or her clients.

STEVEN T. GOLDBERG
BUT WHICH MUTUAL FUNDS? (1998)

Where large sums of money are concerned, it is advisable to trust nobody.

AGATHA CHRISTIE (1890–1976)

———•••———

Banks are an almost irresistable attraction for that element of our society which seeks unearned money.

J. EDGAR HOOVER, DIRECTOR, FBI

———•••———

[Mike] Milken's operation had at its core a basic unethical principle: *The quickest and easiest way to make a lot of money is to borrow it and not pay it back.*

BENJAMIN J. STEIN
A LICENSE TO STEAL (1992)

A clear conscience is far more valuable than money.

ANONYMOUS

A man may be a touch, concentrated, successful money-maker and never contribute to his country anything more than a horrible example.

ROBERT MENZIES

There's a sucker born every minute.

P. T. BARNUM (1810–1891)

10

In the End,
Taxes Take a Bite

The taxpayer—that's someone who works for the federal government but doesn't have to take the civil service examination.

RONALD REAGAN (1911–)

———•••••———

Income tax has made more liars out of the American people than golf has.

WILL ROGERS (1879–1935)

———•••••———

It was as true . . . as turnips is. It was as true . . . as taxes is. And nothing's truer than them.

CHARLES DICKENS
DAVID COPPERFIELD (1849–1850)

I have always paid income tax. I object only when it reaches a stage when I am threatened with having nothing left for my old age—which is due to start next Tuesday or Wednesday.

NOEL COWARD (1899–1973)

———•••———

When there is an income tax, the just man will pay more and the unjust less on the same amount of income.

PLATO (C. 428–348 B.C.)
THE REPUBLIC

It is not a tax bill but a tax relief bill providing relief not for the needy but for the greedy.

FRANKLIN D. ROOSEVELT (1882–1945)
TAX BILL VETO MESSAGE, FEBRUARY 22, 1944

Taxation WITH representation ain't so hot either.

GERALD BARZAN, BRITISH TAX ADVISER

I'm proud of paying taxes. The only thing is—I could be just as proud for half the money.

ARTHUR GODFREY (1907–1983)

Next to being shot at and missed, nothing is quite as satisfying as an income tax refund.

F. J. RAYMOND

All money nowadays seems to be produced with a natural homing instinct for the Treasury.

THE DUKE OF EDINBURGH
OBSERVER SAYINGS (1963)

Unquestionably, there is progress. The average American now pays out twice as much in taxes as he formerly got in wages.

H. L. MENCKEN (1880–1956)

Tax reform means: "Don't tax you, don't tax me. Tax that fellow behind the tree."

RUSSELL LONG, CHAIRMAN OF THE U.S. SENATE
FINANCE COMMITTEE

The art of taxation consists in so plucking the goose as to obtain the largest amount of feathers with the least possible amount of hissing.

JEAN BAPTISTE COLBERT (1619–1683)

The avoidance of taxes is the only intellectual pursuit that carries any reward

JOHN MAYNARD KEYNES (1883–1946)

The collection of any taxes, which are not absolutely required, which do not beyond reasonable doubt contribute to the public welfare, is only a species of legalized larceny.

CALVIN COOLIDGE (1872–1933)
INAUGURAL ADDRESS, MARCH 4, 1925

———•••———

The ancient Egyptians built elaborate fortresses and tunnels and even posted guards at tombs to stop grave robbers. In today's America, we call that estate planning.

BILL ARCHER, HOUSE WAYS & MEANS COMMITTEE CHAIRMAN
NEW YORK TIMES, JUNE 10, 2000

Only little people pay taxes

LEONA HELMSLEY (1921–   )
CONVICTED OF EVADING $1.7 MILLION IN INCOME TAXES.
SHE WAS IMPRISONED FOR 21 MONTHS AND FINED $6.3 MILLION

———•◦•◦•———

The hardest thing in the world to understand is the income tax.

ALBERT EINSTEIN (1879–1955)

———•◦•◦•———

It's not what you make, it's what you keep.

ANONYMOUS

Works and
Authors Quoted

Honore de Balzac (1799–1850)
Eugenie Grandet (1833)

Steven K. Beckner (1951–)
Back From The Brink: The Greenspan Years (1997)

The Bible (King James Version)

Ambrose Bierce (1842–1914)
The Devil's Dictionary (1911)

Todd Buchholz
Market Shock (1999)

Ron Chernow
The House of Morgan (1991)

Charles Dickens (1812–1870)
David Copperfield (1849–1850)
Martin Chuzzlewit (1843–1844)
Sketches by Boz (1836–1837)

Leslie Dunkling and **Adrian Room**
The Guinness Book of Money (1990)

George Eliot (1819–1880)
Adam Bede (1859)

John Kenneth Galbraith
The Affluent Society (1958)
The Great Crash of 1929 (1954)
Money, Whence It Came, Where It Went (1975)

Paul Gibson
Bear Trap: Why Wall Street Doe$n't Work (1993)

Steven T. Goldberg
*But Which Mutual Funds?: How to Pick the Right Ones
 to Achieve Your Financial Dreams* (1998)

Benjamin Graham and David Dodd
Security Analysis (1934)

William Greider
*Secrets of the Temple: How the Federal Reserve Runs
the Country* (1989)

Herbert Hoover
The Great Depression (1929–1941)

Victor Hugo (1802–1885)
Les Miserables (1862)

Robert Kent
Money Talks (1985)

Michael Lewis
The Money Culture (1991)

Peter Lynch with John Rothschild
*One Up on Wall Street: How to Use What You Know
to Make Money in the Market*

Charles Mackay
Extraordinary Popular Delusions & the Madness of Crowds (1852)

Paul A. Samuelson
Economics: An Introductory Approach, Fifth Edition (1961)

George Bernard Shaw (1856–1950)
The Intelligent Woman's Guide to Socialism, Capitalism, Sovietism and Fascism

Adam Smith (1723–1790)
Theory of Moral Sentiments (1976)

Sophocles
Antigone

Boyden Sparkes and **Samuel Taylor Moore**
The Witch of Wall Street: Hetty Green (1935)

Benjamin J. Stein
A License to Steal: The Untold Story of Michael Milken and the Conspiracy to Bilk the Nation (1992)

Robert H. Thomas
Wall Street Wit & Wisdom (1995)

John Train
The Midas Touch (1988)

Eric Tyson
Mutual Fund$ for Dummie$ (1998)

Lloyd Wendt
*The Wall Street Journal: The Story of Dow Jones & the Nation's
Business Newspaper* (1982)

Tom Wolfe
The Bonfire of the Vanities (1987)

Index